The Chrysler Building
The Empire State Building
The First Interstate World Center
The John Hancock Center
NationsBank Plaza

One Liberty Place
The Prudential Tower
The Sears Tower
The Transamerica Pyramid
The World Trade Towers

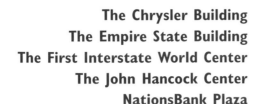

AMERICA'S TOP
10
SKYSCRAPERS

By
Edward Ricciuti

Published by Blackbirch Press, Inc.
260 Amity Road
Woodbridge, CT 06525

©1998 Blackbirch Press, Inc.
First Edition

Printed in the USA

10 9 8 7 6 5 4 3 2 1

Library of Congress Cataloging-in-Publication Data
Ricciuti, Edward R.
    America's top 10 skyscrapers / by Edward R. Ricciuti.
        p. cm.—(America's top 10)
    Includes bibliographical references and index.
    Summary: Describes ten of the most unique and interesting skyscrapers in the United
States including the Empire State Building, the Prudential Center, and the John Hancock
Center.
    ISBN 1-56711-193-9 (lib. bdg. : alk. paper)
    1. Skyscrapers—United States—Juvenile literature. [1. Skyscrapers.] I. Title. II. Series.
NA6232.R5 1998   97–3637
720'.483—dc21   CIP
                                                                                                        AC

BLACKBIRCH PRESS, INC.
WOODBRIDGE, CONNECTICUT

AMERICA'S TOP

10

SKYSCRAPERS

CANADA

NY

VT

ME

NH

MA

CT

RI

PA

NJ

MD

Chrysler
Building

The Chrysler Building

★ ★ ★ ★ ★ ★ ★ ★ ★ ★ ★ ★ ★ ★ ★

When it was completed in 1930, the Chrysler Building, in New York City, was the tallest building in the world. A year later, this 1,046-foot skyscraper was surpassed in height by the nearby Empire State Building. Today, the Chrysler Building is seventh tallest in the United States. The building is not known for its height, however. It is famous for the decorative details extending from its lobby to its peak.

The many design elements in the Chrysler Building were inspired by American automobiles. The reason for this unusual theme is that the building was named after Walter P. Chrysler, the founder of the Chrysler Corporation, which has been manufacturing cars since 1925. The building's exterior is decorated with huge, stainless steel sculptures of automobiles, radiator caps, and eagles. Also on the outside, above the 26th floor, are cars made out of gray and white bricks with steel hubcaps. In the lobby, a mural painted on the ceiling shows scenes from the Chrysler Corporation's factories. The tower on top of the building is made of stainless steel. It is constructed of 6 arcs, one on top of the other.

When it was built, the Chrysler Building contained technical features never before used, such as a central vacuum cleaning system. Called "the city within a city," the building was a self-contained community. Inside were an astonishing number of services: barbershops and beauty parlors, 2 gyms, a restaurant, and even 2 hospital emergency rooms! The Chrysler Building was truly ahead of its time.

Location: New York, New York
Opened: April 1930
Materials: Steel and stone
Height: 1,046 feet
Number of stories: 77
Cost: $15 million
Fun fact: 391,831 rivets, or metal bolts, were used to build the Chrysler Building.

Opposite page:
When the Chrysler Building first opened, one writer described the 6 arcs at the top as 6 sunbursts.

AMERICA'S TOP
10
SKYSCRAPERS

CANADA

VT
ME
NH
NY
MA
CT
RI

PA

NJ

MD

★ Empire
State
Building

★ ★ ★ ★ ★ ★ ★ *The* ★ ★ ★ ★ ★ ★ ★

Empire State Building

In the 1933 movie *King Kong*, the Empire State Building in New York is featured in one of the most memorable scenes of motion picture history. In it, the giant Kong climbs to the very top of the 1,250-foot skyscraper. The Empire State Building had been built 2 years before the movie was made, and was then the world's tallest building. Today it ranks seventh tallest in the world and fourth tallest in the United States.

The Empire State Building was named one of the 7 civil engineering wonders of the world by the American Society of Civil Engineers. Its sleek design set a new standard for the construction of tall buildings. The building's main shaft soars upward, ending in a series of step-like indentations called "setbacks." The slender tower at the top points toward the sky like a giant, metal finger.

The Empire State Building has 102 floors. On the 86th floor is a famous observatory. The building's 73 elevators operate at speeds of 600 to 1,400 feet a minute. On top of the observatory is a transmission tower used by 3 New York City television stations and 17 FM radio stations.

The Empire State Building was so well engineered that its structural safety was not harmed when a U.S. Air Force B-25 bomber crashed into its 79th floor in 1945 on July 28. Only the interior of 2 floors were damaged by the accident.

What may be most remarkable about the Empire State Building is the speed with which this huge structure was built. The workers finished the job in only 1 year and 45 days.

Location: New York, New York
Opened: May 1931
Materials: Aluminum, granite, limestone, steel
Height: Building 1,250 feet; television tower 214 feet
Number of stories: 102
Cost: $40,948
Fun fact: The Empire State Building contains 60,000 tons of steel—enough to build a double-track railroad from New York City to Baltimore.

Opposite page:
The step-like setbacks near the top of the Empire State Building were a revolutionary design.

AMERICA'S TOP

10

SKYSCRAPERS

OR ID

NV

Pacific Ocean CA · UT

First Interstate
World Center ★ AZ

MEXICO

SHERATON
GRANDE

The First Interstate World Center

The First Interstate World Center in Los Angeles, California, is the tallest skyscraper west of Chicago. Since it was opened in 1990, the building has become the most recognized modern landmark in Los Angeles. It has a cylindrical shape that tapers from the base to the peak. Atop the white marble building is a circular glass crown that is illuminated at night. The crown is not simply a decoration. It houses the building's air-conditioning equipment. Above the lobby entrance is a dramatic mural made of metal with images that show scenes from the city's past.

Los Angeles residents often refer to the First Interstate World Center as Library Tower because it stands next to the old Los Angeles Central Library, a landmark that was built in the 1920s. Citizens worried that construction of the First Interstate World Center would require that the library be torn down. That did not happen. Instead, the developers of the new skyscraper worked to restore the old library and even replanted the library lawn, which had been paved over as a parking lot.

The First Interstate World Center was designed to enrich the neighborhood in which it was built. To the west of the north entrance and running alongside the building is a large public space called the Bunker Hill Steps. These spectacular steps were inspired by the Spanish Steps in Rome. They connect two business areas of the city that had been divided by a wall. The First Interstate World Center is proof that a skyscraper can also be a work of art.

Location: Los Angeles, California
Opened: January 1990
Materials: Concrete, marble, steel
Height: 1,108 feet
Number of stories: 73
Cost: $450 million
Fun fact: The Bunker Hill Steps cover a distance of 50 feet.

Opposite page:
The white marble exterior of the First Interstate World Center contrasts with the blue L.A. sky.

AMERICA'S TOP
10
SKYSCRAPERS

WI
IA
John
Hancock
Center
MI
OH
IL
IN
MO
KY

PLAYBOY

The
John Hancock Center

★ ★ ★ ★ ★ ★ ★   ★ ★ ★ ★ ★ ★ ★

The John Hancock Center, in Chicago, stands 1,127 feet high. Its twin 349-foot antennae are used by 8 television stations and 12 radio stations.

The big, black skyscraper is known best for its pioneering structural design. Most skyscrapers are supported by an interior skeleton of steel beams that braces the building against the wind. The outer walls merely hang on the skeleton like a curtain (they are called "curtain walls"). At the John Hancock Center, however, winds are offset by steel braces in the exterior walls. This type of construction uses less steel and increases the amount of interior space.

The outer "skin," or covering, of black aluminum contrasts with the John Hancock Center's many bronze windows, giving it a dramatic appearance. The structure's 1,250 miles of electrical wiring transmit enough power to supply a city of 30,000 people. The actual building takes up only 40 percent of the site on which it stands. The rest of the area is open space—rare in the heart of this city.

This building was constructed for the John Hancock Mutual Insurance Company. In the observatory on the top floor are a number of interesting displays, including a letter written by John Hancock, the first person to sign the Declaration of Independence. Since Chicago residents love their city's professional sports teams, they are also represented in the observatory. On display are a golden bull from the Chicago Bulls basketball team and baseballs autographed by the White Sox and the Cubs.

Location: Chicago, Illinois
Opened: March 1970
Materials: Aluminum, concrete, glass, steel
Height: Building 1,127 feet; antennae 349 feet
Number of stories: 100
Cost: $100 million
Fun fact: The frame of the building contains enough steel to make 33,000 cars.

Opposite page:
The John Hancock Center helped to pioneer a new kind of structural design.

AMERICA'S TOP

10

SKYSCRAPERS

TN

★ NationsBank
Plaza

SC

AL

GA

FL

The
NationsBank Plaza

★ ★ ★ ★ ★ ★ ★ ★ ★ ★ ★ ★

During the 1980s and early 1990s, the skyline of Atlanta, Georgia, underwent striking changes. Skyscrapers began to rise with amazing speed, like mushrooms popping out of the ground after a rainstorm. The tallest of these buildings is the NationsBank Plaza, which was completed in February 1992. It was a massive construction job and was finished in a surprisingly short time. The 1,023-foot-high building required 24,000 tons of steel and 68,400 cubic yards of concrete. It took 17,000 truckloads to remove the earth that was excavated from the building site. Workers called the building schedule the "blast track"—even faster than the "fast track!" Only 2 years after construction began, the first tenants were moving into the building—a remarkable achievement. The architects worked closely with the contractor—the person who supervised the construction process—in order to complete the project quickly.

The NationsBank Plaza is supported by what architects call "super columns." Each column is made of a steel frame encased in concrete. All 8 of the super columns are located on the outside of the building. By placing the building's supporting structures entirely on the exterior, designers provided for more usable space inside. The outside of the building is an aluminum framework that holds red granite and bronze-tinted windows. Atop the roof is a steel cage that resembles a pyramid with steps. At night, the cage is illuminated and can be seen for miles.

Location: Atlanta, Georgia
Opened: February 1992
Materials: Concrete, granite, steel
Height: 1,023 feet
Number of stories: 55
Cost: $117 million
Fun fact: The construction schedule called for 4 days of work per floor. It was shortened to 3 per floor.

Opposite page:
The NationsBank building was designed to have 8 supporting columns on its exterior.

AMERICA'S TOP

10

SKYSCRAPERS

CANADA

NY

PA

One
Liberty
Place

NJ

OH

MD

DE

WV

VA

One Liberty Place

In 1986, on September 10, William Penn's 3-cornered hat was no longer the highest point in Philadelphia, Pennsylvania. Until that day, it was a custom in Philadelphia that no building should be taller than the statue of William Penn, which stands atop City Hall. (Penn was the Colonial leader who founded Philadelphia.) The tradition was broken, however, when a construction-crane operator lifted the first of several steel columns used to frame the 44th floor of One Liberty Place. When One Liberty Place was completed, the 959-foot building was almost double the height of "Billy Penn's" statue.

One Liberty Place is not only taller than any building in Philadelphia—it has a different shape. Most tall buildings in the city have flat tops. One Liberty Place is crowned by a glass pyramid, topped by a spire.

Like NationsBank Plaza, One Liberty Place is supported by a dozen "super columns." Four of these columns form a rectangular core in the center of the building. The other columns are on the outside of the building, 2 of them on each of the 4 walls. The exterior of One Liberty Place is covered by granite and glass. The base is completely clad in granite. As the building increases in height, more glass is used in place of granite. Finally, at the top, the building is all glass. The architects felt that this transition from stone to glass mirrored the change in landscape from earth to sky.

Location: Philadelphia, Pennsylvania
Opened: February 1988
Materials: Concrete, glass, granite, steel
Height: 945 feet
Number of stories: 61
Cost: $200 million
Fun fact: One Liberty Place has 28 elevators.

Opposite page:
The graceful pyramid and spire atop One Liberty Place contrast with the surrounding flat-topped buildings.

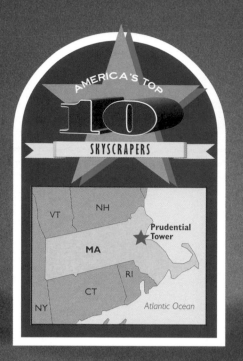

AMERICA'S TOP

10

SKYSCRAPERS

VT NH

MA
★ Prudential
Tower

RI
CT

NY Atlantic Ocean

SHERATON

The
Prudential Tower

★ ★ ★ ★ ★ ★ ★ ★ ★ ★ ★ ★ ★ ★

The Prudential Tower, in Boston, Massachusetts, crowns an indoor shopping mall. The mall is surrounded by an outdoor plaza. Together, the plaza, mall, and tower are referred to as the Prudential Center. Standing 750 feet high, not including its television mast, the tower has a total of 10 acres, or 435,600 square feet of glass—a large amount for a building of its size. Two million fasteners were required to seal the 10,000 windows in place. Although it is not the tallest building in Boston—the John Hancock Center is 38 feet higher—Prudential Tower is recognized by most Bostonians as the most significant structure in the city. They often refer to it as the "Pru."

The Prudential Center and its tower were built over the Conrail railroad tracks and the Massachusetts Turnpike—a major road that crosses much of the state. To allow the tracks and highway to run beneath the site, the center was raised 18 feet above street level. The center's parking garage was split into two sections by the tracks and turnpike.

The tower itself, topped by 13-foot-high letters that spell "Prudential," is visible far beyond the city limits. The walls of this rectangular building are 150 by 178 feet wide. The structural steel that forms the internal skeleton of the tower weighs 60 million pounds. The building's foundations reach 170 feet below the ground.

Today, the Prudential Tower is considered to be as much a Boston landmark as Fenway Park, home of the Red Sox baseball team.

Location: Boston, Massachusetts
Opened: September 8, 1964
Materials: Concrete and steel
Height: 750 feet
Number of stories: 52
Cost: $200 million
Fun fact: The elevators take only 30 seconds to reach the observation deck on the 50th floor.

Opposite page:
The Prudential Tower is reflected on the Charles River.

AMERICA'S TOP
10
SKYSCRAPERS

WI
IA
Sears
Tower
MI
OH
IL
IN
MO
KY

Harrison
HOTEL
PARK FREE

TORCO

★ ★ ★ ★ ★ ★ ★ *The* ★ ★ ★ ★ ★ ★ ★

Sears Tower

Until the middle of the 1990s, the Sears Tower, in Chicago, was recognized as the world's tallest building. Then construction of the Petronas Twin Towers in Malaysia changed the rank of the Sears Tower to Number 2, according to the Council on Tall Buildings and Urban Habitat.

The tower, at 1,454 feet high, is nevertheless one of the most impressive structures ever built. Everything about it is big. In a city of massive buildings, it stands well above the others. The Sears Tower has 110 stories with 4.5 million feet of floor space, the equivalent of 101 acres! The tower has 16,100 bronze-tinted windows, which are washed by 6 machines mounted on the roof. The bronzed windows contrast with the tower's outer wall of black aluminum, giving the building a spectacular exterior. The tower contains 76,000 tons of structural steel—enough to build more than 52,000 automobiles. The 104 elevators in the building operate at a speed of up to 1,600 feet a minute. They are among the fastest in the world.

The tower was originally built to house the headquarters of Sears, Roebuck and Co. Its design was completed in July 1970 and construction began a month later. By September 1973, the first Sears employees began moving into the building. Nine years later, the antennae atop the structure were completed. They are used by more than 20 radio and TV stations. After Sears moved its headquarters to the Chicago suburbs in 1993, the tower was renovated to accommodate many other companies and organizations.

Location: Chicago, Illinois
Opened: 1973
Materials: Aluminum, concrete, glass, steel
Height: 1,454 feet, antennae 253 feet
Number of stories: 110
Cost: Over $150 million
Fun fact: The Sears Tower has 25,000 miles of plumbing pipe and 2,000 miles of electrical wire.

Opposite page:
The tall antennae of the Sears Tower seem to pierce the sky.

AMERICA'S TOP
10
SKYSCRAPERS

OR
ID
NV
UT
Transamerica
Pyramid
CA
AZ
Pacific Ocean
MEXICO

The
Transamerica Pyramid

The Transamerica Pyramid, in San Francisco, is one of the most striking skyscrapers in the world. It is a slender structure that is shaped like a pyramid with a pair of windowless wings rising up from the 29th floor. Although some of the city's residents did not like the building at first, it has become a landmark that is admired by San Francisco's visitors and residents alike.

The designers of the pyramid patterned the building after the famous redwood trees of northern California. Like the tall redwoods, the building tapers as its height increases. This design allows more light to reach the streets than the design of rectangular skyscrapers. Once the pyramid was opened, it became a popular place to visit. Next door is the Transamerica Redwood Park, a half-acre site on which redwoods have been planted.

The pyramid is also noted for its many safety features. In particular, it was built to withstand strong earthquakes. While skyscrapers usually rest on pilings sunk into the earth, the pyramid stands on a slab of concrete 9 feet thick. Automatic water sprinklers for fighting fires were installed on each floor, and in the building's west wing, there is a shaft that allows smoke to escape. The other wing contains an elevator shaft that serves the higher floors.

Since it was opened, the pyramid has been featured on postcards, in movies, and on television. It has become one of the best-known landmarks of San Francisco.

Location: San Francisco, California
Opened: August 1972
Materials: Concrete and steel
Height: 853 feet
Number of stories: 48
Cost: $43 million
Fun fact: The Transamerica Pyramid has 3,678 windows.

Opposite page:
The unusual design of the Transamerica Pyramid was inspired by redwood trees.

AMERICA'S TOP

10

SKYSCRAPERS

CANADA

VT
ME
NH
NY
MA
CT
PA
NJ
MD

★ World
Trade
Center

The
World Trade Towers

The World Trade Center, in New York City, is a complex of 7 buildings, including the famed twin towers—the second- and third-tallest buildings in America. The tower at One World Trade Center rises 1,368 feet—6 feet higher than its twin. Each tower is so large that it has its own individual postal ZIP code!

This huge building complex was commissioned, or ordered, by the Port Authority of New York and New Jersey, the transportation agency for the two states. Excavation of the site, which began in 1966, took 2 years. More than 1.2 million cubic yards of earth and rock had to be removed before the buildings' steel frames could be constructed. The base of each center weighed 1.3 million tons, and required 425,000 cubic yards of concrete—enough to build a sidewalk from New York City to Washington, D.C.

The design of the twin towers included a pioneering advance in skyscraper construction that was also used in Chicago's John Hancock Center. Up to that point, the typical skyscraper of the period had an internal skeleton of steel columns. This skeleton supported the weight and braced against the wind. Most of the steel in the twin towers, however, is on the outside, which increases the amount of usable space within.

In 1993, on February 26, a terrorist bomb exploded at the World Trade Center. It killed 6 people and injured more than 1,000. Both towers were extensively damaged, but repairs were made quickly, and they were reopened a month later.

Location: New York, New York
Opened: December 1970
Materials: Concrete and steel
Height: Tower One 1,368 feet; television mast 360 feet; Tower Two 1,362 feet
Number of stories: 110 in each tower
Cost: $800 million
Fun fact: The Top of the World observation deck in Tower Two draws 1.8 million visitors per year.

Opposite page:
The twin towers of the World Trade Center soar above the older buildings of lower Manhattan.

America's Top 10 Skyscrapers are not necessarily the highest. Although height was one basis for including a building in this volume, we also considered a skyscraper's cultural and architectural significance. Below is a list of 10 other notable skyscrapers.

More American Skyscrapers

Building, Height, *Location*

American International Building, 950 feet, *New York, New York*

Amoco Building, 1,136 feet, *Chicago, Illinois*

Citicorp Center, 915 feet, *New York, New York*

Columbia Seafirst Center, 943 feet, *Seattle, Washington*

First Interstate Bank Plaza, 972 feet, *Houston, Texas*

40 Wall Street, 927 feet, *New York, New York*

John Hancock Center, 788 feet, *Boston, Massachusetts*

Texas Commerce Tower, 1,000 feet, *Houston, Texas*

311 South Wacker Drive, 959 feet, *Chicago, Illinois*

Transco Tower, 901 feet, *Houston, Texas*

Two Prudential Plaza, 978 feet, *Chicago, Illinois*

Glossary

bedrock The solid rock that is found beneath the surface of the earth.

clad Completely covered.

illuminated Brightened with light.

pilings Long columns of steel, wood, or concrete that are driven into the ground to support the weight of a heavy structure.

pyramid A building design that was used in ancient Egypt. The outside walls form 4 triangles that come together in a point at the top.

restore To bring back to its original state.

shaft In this book, part of a structure shaped like a long column.

Further Reading

Conlin, Stephen. *Fold-out Skyscrapers*. Skokie, IL: Rand McNally, 1995.

Doherty, Craig and Katherine Doherty. *Building America: The Sears Tower*. Woodbridge, CT: Blackbirch Press, 1995.

————. *Building America: The Empire State Building*. Woodbridge, CT: Blackbirch Press, 1998.

Duncan, Michael. *How Skyscrapers Are Made*. New York: Facts On File, 1987.

Dunn, Andrew. *Skyscrapers*. New York: Thomson Learning, 1993.

Gibbons, Gail. *Up Goes the Skyscraper!* New York: Simon and Schuster Children, 1986.

Where to Get On-Line Information

Empire State Building	http://www.nyctourist.com/empire1.htm
One Liberty Place	http://www.gim.net/libertyplace
Sears Tower	http://www.fadc.com/new.htm/#2
Transamerica Pyramid	http://www.cityinsights.com/sftransa.htm
World Trade Center	http://www.wtca.org/wtc/new_york.html

Index

Photo Credits

Cover and pages 2, 4, 20: ©Blackbirch Press; cover and page 6: Courtesy of the Los Angeles Convention and Visitors Bureau/©1991 Michele and Tom Grimm; cover and page 8: ©Leo de Wys/Leo dy Wys, Inc.; cover and page 10: Courtesy of Beers Construction Company; cover and page 12: Superstock Photo, Inc.; cover and page 14: George F. Mobley/National Geographic Image Collection; cover and page 16: ©1992 PeterSkinner/Photo Researchers, Inc.; cover and page 18: San Francisco Convention and Visitors Bureau photo by Kerrick James.